The

H.O.L.O.

Brothers

The H.O.L.D. Brothers

THE CURSE OF THE BLOATED TOAD

by Jim Rohn

FANTAGRAPHICS BOOKS

FANTAGRAPHICS BOOKS
1800 Bridgegate St., Suite #101,
Westlake Village, CA 91361

Editor: Gary Groth
Art Direction: Dale Crain,
Coco Shinomiya, Jim Rohn
Typesetting: Kim Thompson

First Fantagraphics Books edition:
February 1988.
1 2 3 4 5 6 7 8 9 10

ISBN: 0-930193-36-9.

Printed in the U.S.A.

Well, here it is. It was almost three years ago that Gary, Jay, Mike, Dave, and I started hammering out the package that would eventually become *Threat!* I thought *The Holo. Brothers* would inject some humor, satire, and solid character development into a genre littered with cliches. What *hasn't* been done in science fiction comics, right? I hope that *The Holo. Brothers* is a unique enough blend of disparate influences—space opera, vaudeville, art deco, and a smart-ass mentality—to make for an enjoyable romp.

Time sure flies, though. It's a bit disconcerting to see how quickly two years of work can be read. You hold in your hands some 80-odd pages, and yet, as anyone in this industry will tell you, that number is deceiving. For every page of finished art that gets printed, many hours are invested in sketches, tracings, and plain old screw-ups. I won't even go into all the time spent "just thinking" about plots, or how much time went into the cover art.

But before we begin, the "I'd like to thank the Academy" scene. Sure, I know it's corny, but if *you* can resist thanking the people who've helped out when you get *your* first book, you're a better man than I. In no coherent order—

You. Holding this book. Whoever you are. After all, most of us are drawn to this profession by the urge to relate or communicate ideas. Without the readers, I might as well sit on a park bench somewhere babbling to myself. Believe me, your support and interest are very much appreciated. Unless you're reading this in a book store, in which case put it back, because this is not a library.

Gary Groth and the whole Fantagraphics crew. I've received nothing but support from them over the past two years and I'm looking forward to working with them on the (plug time) forthcoming five-part *Holo. Brothers* series—plus a bonus 30-page "origin issue."

It's funny. Over the last six years or so, a lot of so-called alternative publishers have cropped up, but more often than not it's just different people producing more of the same. I think Gary is dedicated to pushing the boundaries of comics to their limits and I'm happy to be a part of that.

The Pros. Those guys who have, by example, led me down the path of cartooning: Neal Adams, Hal Foster, Walt Kelly, Chuck Jones, Jack Kirby, John Buscema, Gil Kane, Jeff MacNelly, Howard Chaykin, Bill Sienkiewicz, Frank Miller, Walt Simonson—well, hell, this could go on forever.

My partners in crime, either in Joisey or Chicago, who have been sounding boards for ideas and have critiqued my work (sometimes unasked!) in an effort to make it the best possible. Especially the other Threat Boys. Also a special double secret thanks to Gary Fields for the lettering job.

My family. I've got one of each: brother, sister, mother, father, and almost every page highlights some interest I share with one or all of them. I'm very fortunate to have been brought up in a home where creativity was a given and talent was always appreciated.

And speaking of family, a special thanks and dedication to my wife-to-be! You see, this introduction is the last piece of business required before I head East to take the matrimonial plunge. Before I do, I'd like to say that Mary Ann has been a constant source of strength and support and a real joy to be with.

Whew! Not a dry eye in the house, eh? Well, I figure that in a book with 85 pages of cynicism, a little sentimentality wouldn't kill you. Hope you have had run reading this, and I'll see you in the funny papers.   —JIM ROHN, April 1987

"IN OLDEN DAYS A GLIMPSE OF STOCKING WAS LOOKED ON AS SOMETHING SHOCKING..."

"NOW, HEAVEN KNOWS--ANYTHING GOES,"

"GOOD AUTHORS, TOO, WHO ONCE KNEW BETTER WORDS NOW ONLY USE FOUR LETTER WORDS WRITING PROSE,..."

"ANYTHING GOES"

strokes 'n' stuff!!!

BABES SEX!
DEEP GOAT
HOS 'B' US
CRIMES!
"barnyard buddies"
TEENAGE NINJA CHEERLEADERS IN BONDAGE!
HOT
•DONNA MATRIX
SEX! SEX! SEX!
GOILS GOILS GO
EMBRACABLE EWE!
LUST

"THE WORLD HAS GONE MAD TODAY."

"AND GOOD'S BAD TODAY,"

"AND BLACK'S WHITE TODAY,"

"AND DAY'S NIGHT TODAY,"

"WHEN MOST GUYS TODAY THAT WOMEN PRIZE TODAY...."

"ARE SILLY GIGOLOS,"

DON'T

The H.O.L.O. Brothers

BROUGHT TO YOU BY— JIM ROHN and GARY FIELDS

SCRIPT & ART / LETTERS

LYRICS BY COLE PORTER

FIRST...THERE HAD BEEN..."THE BOOM"- AN EXPANSION OF TECHNOLOGY AND INTERSTELLAR COLONIZATION UNHEARD OF IN HISTORY.

THE PEOPLE PROSPERED AND THE WAY OF 'THE GREAT MACHINES' WAS SPREAD THROUGHOUT THE GALAXY.

THEN CAME... "THE BUST"... THE ANCIENT FUELS USED BY THE MACHINES RAN OUT AND THE SYSTEM COLLAPSED.

THE STREET PEOPLE ABANDONED THE RULES OF THE STATE AND FOUND SOLACE IN 'THE ORDER OF THE GEM'- A RELIGION DEIFYING THE JEWELS USED TO REKINDLE THE GREAT MACHINES.

AN UNEASY ALLIANCE WAS FORMED BETWEEN THE GOVERNMENT AND THE BLACK MARKET, KEEPING THE LIGHTS ON HOMEWORLD BURNING BRIGHTLY.

GALS ~ STUFF

THE C'MON INN

OUR GIRLS ARE BOX

PIX·PIX

THEN ONE NIGHT, THE LAST SACRED JEWEL WAS STOLEN-AND ONCE AGAIN, THE LIGHTS ON HOMEWORLD BEGAN TO DIM.

"I DON' BELIEVE THIS!!"

"KNOCK IT OFF, T.K."

The STRIPED APE

"'EASY MONEY' YOU SAID!"

"'EASY MONEY' DIOS MIO!!"

"PLAYING WHEEL MAN TO TWO SMART-ASS CON MEN... THAT ES NOT "EASY MONEY", LARRY!!!... THAT ES *Certain Trouble!!*

YOU'RE RANTING—YOU KNOW THAT?

I GO WAY BACK WITH THESE GUYS, **TEQUILA**—GRANTED, **MAX** IS SHORT ON ETHICS, BUT HE KNOWS THE STREETS! AND **JERRY** CAN TAKE CARE OF HIMSELF... **BELIEVE ME!!**

DO YOU KNOW WHAT YOU GET FOR ESTEALING PALACE JEWELS?! NO WAIT, AMIGO... I'LL...TELL...YOU...

you get killed!! KILLED QUICK IF YOU'RE LUCKY!

YOU AN' YOUR FRIENDS END UP OZONE AND I GET TURNED INTO PRIME PARTS!!

I CAN ALWAYS SPEND **YOUR** SHARE IF YOU WANT TO BOW OUT!!

WELL NO BUT...

THEN WILL YOU SIT BACK AND RELAX? THIS SHOULD BE GOOD!!

7

TRY TO DRUM UP SOME BUSINESS. I'LL KEEP BUSY!

NO **SKIRTS**, JERRY... JUST KEEP YOUR EYES PEELED!

...FROZEN JOVIAN DAQUIRI, CHUCKLES, EXTRA RED SPOT... 'N' I'LL SLIDE YA AN EXTRA **C-NOTE** IF YA KNOW WHERE I CAN MOVE SOME HOT MERCHANDISE!

DEPENDS... WHADDYA GOT?

A LITTLE ICE I PICKED UP AT THE IMPERIAL PALACE!

"THE EYE OF THE BLOATED TOAD"!?

YOU DISAPPOINT ME, MAX.

STUPID! STUPID!

HERR LIPPMAN!

YOU SHOULD KNOW "DER STRIPED APE" IS DER **FIRST** PLACE I VOULD LOOK!

NOW HAND OVER THE CHEWELL, UND VE VILL...

NOT A **CHANCE** PAL! YOU AND YOUR FLUNKIES ARE CAT CHOW NOW!

HOLD IT, FUZZBALL!

WHAT THE...?

LISTEN TO TH' MAN!

UNLIKE YOU, I BROUGHT SUFFICIENT MUSCLE TO BACK ME UP!
I'LL TAKE DER CHEWELL NOW!
I...I CAN EXPLAIN EVERYTHING FRANZ... THE JOB, THE GUARDS, YOUR EYE... IT WAS ALL A MISTAKE!
HMM...
VE BOTH MADE MISTAKES, HOLOGRAM... I SHOULDN'T HAFF TEAMED UP VIT YOU ON DIS JOB IN DER FIRST PLACE! UND YOU... SHOULDN'T HAFF LEFT ME TO FIGHT DER GUARDS ALONE! IT COST ME AN EYE, MAX...
UND IT VILL COST YOU... YOUR LIFE!
VOT DER?!...
ZZZZT!
ZZZZT!
KREEEGAAH!!...

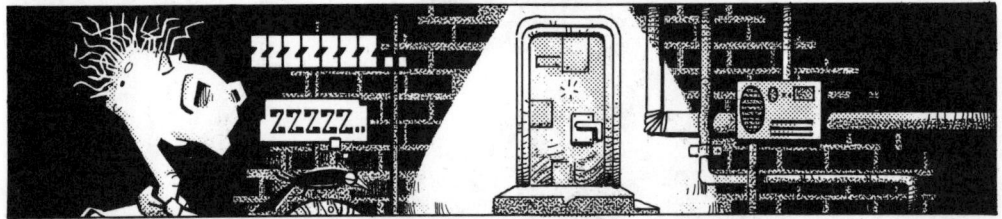

End of Chapter 1

12

ABOVE...

...THEREFORE, POWER LEVELS SHOULD SHOW NO DISCERNABLE DROP FOR APPROXIMATELY 4.72 HOURS...

...I THOUGHT A PRESS STATEMENT DETAILING THE...

THERE WILL BE **NO ANNOUNCEMENT** CONCERNING THE JEWEL'S DISAPPEARANCE... ...AS WITH MY **ILLNESS,** THE NEWS WOULD PROVE TOO CHAOTIC...AND CHAOS IS THE **ONE** THING THIS ADMINISTRATION WOULD NOT SURVIVE.

LOCATE, TRY AND **EXECUTE** THE THIEVES AND REPLACE THE JEWEL QUICKLY BEFORE THERE IS PANIC IN THE STREETS.

AND GEKKUS...

SIR?

I'VE TOLD YOU **BEFORE,** MY **SON** IS TO BE PRESENT AT BRIEFINGS SUCH AS THESE.

IT IS HE WHO IS NEXT IN COMMAND, NOT YOU...

...IS THAT UNDERSTOOD?

PERFECTLY, YOUR HIGHNESS.

1

STOP SHTARINK YOU SVINE...UND HELP ME UP!!

TARGETECH LASER SIGHTING... AND YOU MISSED!?!

WE LOST HIM, RIGHT? THAT'S WHAT COUNTS!

HOW'S MAX'S HAND?!

MY HAND IS THE LEAST OF OUR PROBLEMS, GUYS... HEAD FOR THE SPACE DOCK IN SECTOR 2B... QUICK!! BEFORE THE FEDS CATCH ON!

THE FEDS!? WHAT DO THEY HAVE TO DO WITH THIS!?!

I HAVE A SICK FEELING MAX HASN'T TOLD US EVERYTHING, LARRY.

SI, LIKE WHAT GOOD ES THIS ESPACE DOCK WHEN WE DON' EVEN HAVE AN ESPACE SHIP!?!

"DON'T HAVE A SHIP," EH? HELL, T.K., THAT'S THE EASIEST PART!!

IMPERIAL SPACE DOCK 2B TRESPASSIN IS NOT TOLERA

"WE JUMP A GUARD..."

"BLAST THE HATCH..."

"HOTWIRE THE DASH..."

...AND WE'RE AIRBORNE!! SEE? IT'S A SNAP!

"A SNAP"? HA! YOU'RE A RIOT, MAX!

4

...OUT OF HOMEWORLD'S JURISDICTION IN 6 SECONDS FLAT!! SAFE AT LAST!!

WISHFUL THINKING, TEQUILA, LOOK WHAT'S COMING OUR WAY!!

MADRE MIA!! A STAR SCOUT!

WE'RE DEAD!! FINITO!!!

ATTENTION JC32:........ ...UNIDENTIFIED SHIP VIOLATING MOON'S AIR SPACE... ...INVESTIGATE AND INTERCEPT.....

LIPPMAN!! CAN YOU IMAGINE THAT DAMN CAT CRIPPLIN' ME LIKE THIS !?!

I CAN'T IMAGINE YOU THINKING YOU COULD GET AWAY WITH SHAFTING SOMEONE LIKE HIM ON A JEWEL HEIST. YOU'RE LUCKY YOU WEREN'T KILLED!!

THERE MUST BE SOMETHING BACK HERE I CAN USE TO FIX YOUR HAND.

MAYBE THIS CRATE HAS WHAT WE... OH GREAT!!.. GUESS WHAT, MAX...

...WE HAVE OURSELVES A STOWAWAY!!

⑤

17

ONE SHIP!?! DON'T INSULT ME, BIRD... LET ME SHOW YOU WHAT I LEARNED IN THE PERIMETER SQUAD!!

"YOU START WITH A SIMPLE TWO-STEP..."

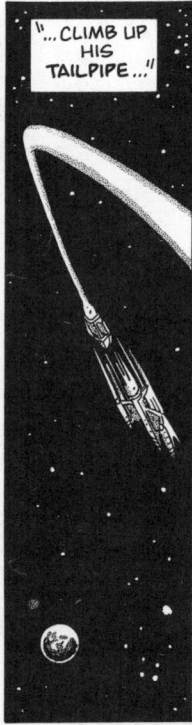

"...CLIMB UP HIS TAILPIPE..."

...PAUSE A MOMENT FOR REFLECTION...

...AND THEN BLAST THE HELL OUTTA THEM!!

...APPROACHING FREIGHTER... REFUSES TO RETURN CODE...   ...MANEUVERING FOR ATTACK....   ...HE'S ON MY TAIL! I NEED ASSIST.......

A STOWAWAY, HUH? AND I THOUGHT IT COULDN'T GET ANY WORSE...COME CLEAN, KID... YOU GOT A STORY?

I WORK... WORKED AT THE IMPERIAL PALACE, MAINTENANCE, LOW LEVEL SECURITY.

YOU KNOW, GRUNT WORK!

ANYWAY... LAST NIGHT THE IMPERIAL JEWEL WAS STOLEN... CAUSED A REAL STIR.

THEY'RE SCREENING ALL PERSONNEL, TRYING TO FIND A SCAPEGOAT AND WITH MY BACKGROUND I'M TAILOR-MADE FOR THE JOB...

...SO I SPLIT!!

I DON'T HAVE ANY FAMILY OR FRIENDS, SO I HID IN HERE UNTIL YOU SHOWED UP!

SO SOMEONE STOLE THE IMPERIAL JEWEL, EH?... SOUND FAMILIAR, MAX?

STOW IT, LAR. LOOK KID... WE'RE RUNNING FROM THE HEAT TOO, SO WE WON'T SQUEAL ON YA!...

...JUST TRY STAYIN' OUTTA THE WAY, OK?

6

BOOM!

SHAKA! LAKA!

NOT BAD, EH? I CAN SEE YOU'RE IM-PRESSED BEYOND MERE WORDS!

"HOKEY SMOKES!! A FREAKIN' IMPERIAL SQUADRON!!"

L...LOOK STUPIDO MIRA, ALLI!! **ALLI!!**

...JC32'S TRANSMISSION HAS ENDED... ...SQUADRON IN PURSUIT... ...TARGET SPOTTED... ...TARGET IN FIRING RANGE...

YOU'RE "ALL HEART", MAX, NOW STAND STILL! THIS BRACE SHOULD HELP UNTIL I CAN GET THE RIGHT EQUIPMENT.

MAX!

WHO'S THAT!?!

THAT'S JERRY!! AND HE NEVER YELLS LIKE THAT...

...UNLESS HE'S IN DEEP SH—

MY THOUGHTS EXACTLY, MAX!!

BRACE YOURSELVES COMPAÑEROS!!...

7

19

IN THE CHAMBERS OF **LORD GEKKUS,** ADMINISTRATIVE ASSISTANT TO THE EMPEROR...

ONLY **HERR LIPP-MAN,** SIR...HE'S BEEN WAITING TO SEE YOU ALL MORNING.

...AND IN-FORM THE MEDIA THAT I SHALL BE RELEASING A **NEWS ITEM** THIS AFTERNOON OF VITAL **CONCERN** TO THE EMPIRE'S WELFARE.

THEN SEND HIM IN, BY ALL MEANS!

YES, M'LORD. WILL THE **EMPEROR** BE **PRESENT?**

I THINK **NOT.** GIVEN HIS **ILLNESS,** I SEE NO REASON TO DIS-**TURB** HIM.

ANY **OTHER** BUSINESS?

AH...**LIPPMAN,** I TRUST YOU HAVE **GOOD** NEWS THIS TIME!

JA, LORD GEKKUS. I HAFF RECOV-ERED **DER CHEWELL** AS PROMISED!

GOOD... VERY GOOD.

AND WHAT OF YOUR "ASSOCIATE"?

DEAD, SIRE. DER SHIP DER **HOLO BROS.** STOLE VAS **TERMI-NATED** UND DER REMAINS CRASHED ON DER **MOON!!**

THE **MOON!?!** ARE YOU SURE THAT THEY WERE **KILLED!?!**

WHA!?!... I...I **ASSUME** SO, M'LORD-- HOW COULD **ANYONE** SUR-VIVE SUCH A CRASH?!

IT'S NOT YOUR PLACE TO ASSUME, LIPP-MAN, BUT TO **OBEY!!** NOW...TAKE MY SCOUTING TEAM AND CHECK THE CRASH SITE **PERSONALLY!!**

COME BACK **CERTAIN...**OR NOT AT ALL!!

21

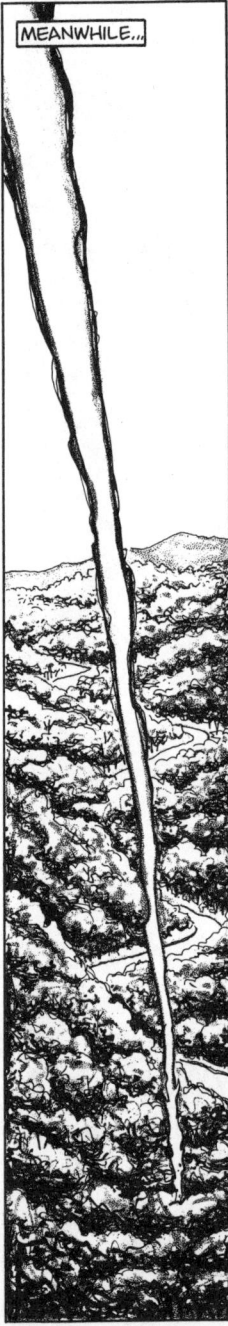

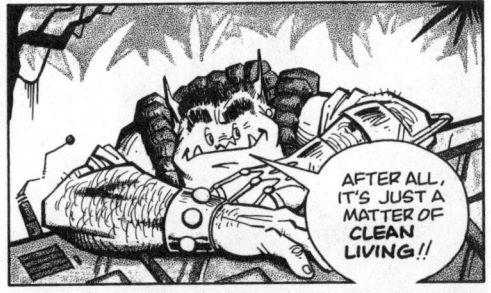

CLEAN LIVING? **DUMB LUCK'S** MORE LIKE IT...Y'KNOW IT'S NO WONDER YOU DON'T BOTHER TO **THINK, MAX**...NOT WITH THE **BREAKS YOU** GET!!

SO WHAT'S YOUR **POINT,** LARRY?

MY POINT IS THAT WE'VE BEEN KNEE-DEEP IN **TROUBLE** FOR THE LAST SIX HOURS AND **I** WANT SOME EXPLANATIONS!

YOU'LL GET MORE THAN **THAT** IF YOU DON'T QUIT **LEAN-**IN' ON ME, PAL...

HEY, **LIGHTEN UP** GUYS!...YOU KNOW IT TAKES **MORE** THAN ONE ROUGH NIGHT TO RUB OUT THE **HOLO** BROTHERS!!

"THE **HOLO** BROTHERS"? WHO ARE **THEY**?!

WHERE'VE YOU **BEEN,** KID? THAT'S **US**!... MAX, JERRY AND LARRY **HOLO-**GRAM!!

"HOLO" FOR SHORT!

YEAH, LIKE ON **WANTED** POSTERS!

AS LONG AS WE'RE ON THE SUBJECT, CHICO, MY NAME IS TE-QUILA MOCK-INGBIRD!...

...BUT YOU CAN CALL ME T.K. ¿COMO SE LLAMA?

MY NAME'S KEVIN, T.K.!

OK, OK,...IF EVERYONE'S **DONE** WITH THE FORMAL-ITIES, LET'S SEE IF THERE'S ANY **ACTION** ON THIS **LUNAR** "PLAYGROUND"!!

23

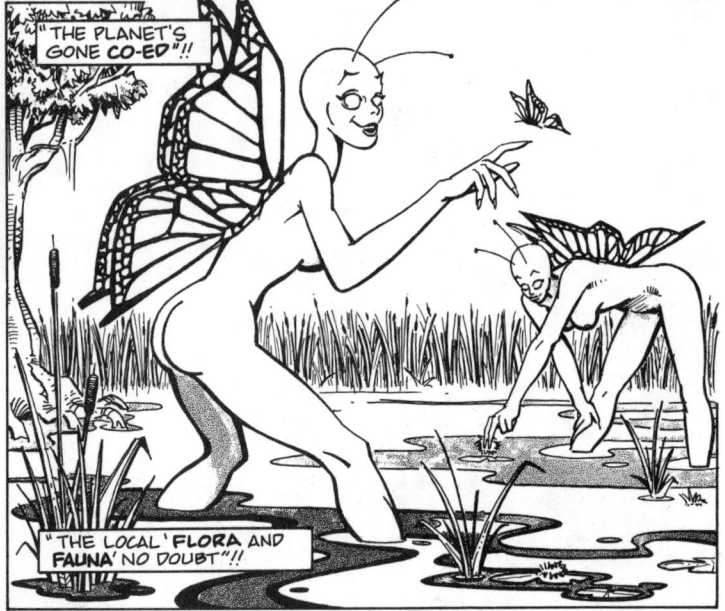

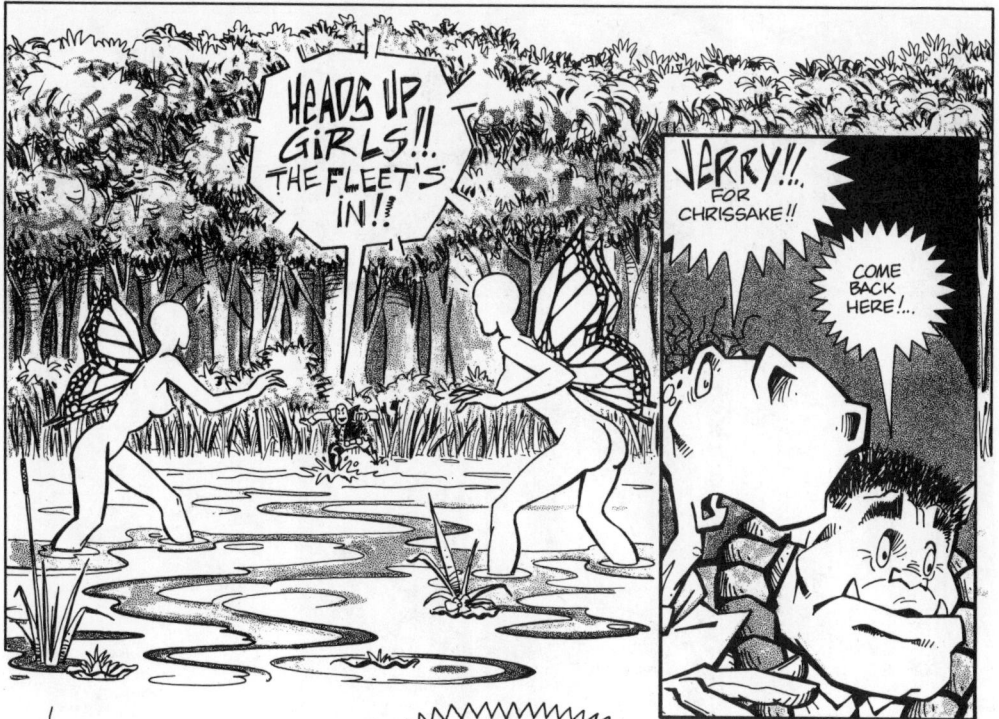

WE'RE ...&PUFF&... ...LOSING... &GASP&... ...HIM...

I ...&WHEEZE&... DIDN'T KNOW... &HUFF&... THE BIG GUY...&PUFF&... COULD RUN SO... &GASP&...FAST!

SPLISH
SPLASH

JUST... &GASP&...SHOWS WHAT... &HUFF&... YOU'RE CAPABLE OF... &WHEEZE&...IN THE MIDDLE OF...&PANT&... A "HORMONE"...&PUFF& "RUSH"!!

Y'KNOW... &GASP& AFTER ALL THIS...&HUFF& ...TROUBLE... I... JUST MIGHT... &WHEEZE&...TAKE ONE OF THOSE BABES MY...

SNIP

...SELLLLFF!!*

DAMMIT!! I SHOULD HAVE KNOWN!! THE WHOLE THING WAS A SET- UP!!

YEAH... AND GUESS WHO RIGGED IT!!

"IT'S A TRIBE OF... BUSHTOADS!!"

26

ON THE MOON OF HOMEWORLD... ABOVE THE JUNGLE TREES... A BLACK FIGURE CIRCLES... **SEARCHING FOR...**

¡KEVIN!! You're not gon' believe wass hoppened!

Sí, I **FOUND** them alright... but let me tell **YOU**...

WHAT IS IT, **TEQUILA**? DID YOU FIND THE **HOLO BROTHERS**?

...**LARRY** AND THE OTHERS HAVE BEEN IN **TROUBLE** BEFORE...

...BUT THIS TIME THEY'VE **OUTDONE** THEMSELVES!

I'LL ESPLAIN AS WE GO... WE DON' HAVE **MUCH TIME**!!

MIRA, AMIGO... ¿ **SEE** WHA HOPPENS WHEN YOU'RE NOT **CAREFUL**? ¿ **SEE** WHA HOPPENS WHEN YOU **CHASE** THE **CHICAS**? SEE? SEE?!!

I **SEE** T.K.- **MAX**, **JERRY** AND **LARRY** HAVE BEEN CAPTURED BY SOME SORT OF..."TOADS"?

BUSH TOADS, **KEVIN**, AND IF WE CAN'T GET "**LOS HOLOS**" OUT OF THERE IMMEDIAMENTE THEY'RE GONNA BE...

28

The HOLO Brothers IN TOADBUSTERS

DEAD MEAT!! IT'S NOT BAD ENOUGH GETTING **STRANDED** ON THIS MOON... NO, WE GOTTA GET **CAPTURED** BY SOME FREAKIN' PREHISTORIC **FROGGIES**!!

YEAH, AND THE WAY THEY'RE DANCING AROUND PROBABLY MEANS THAT WE'RE THE "HOLO DU JOUR" ON THEIR MENU!

LARRY, HAVE YOU FIGURED OUT WHAT THEIR CHIEF IS SAYING?

JIM RAIN
SCRIPT & ART
GARY FIELDS-
LETTERING

I CAN'T TELL. IT'S SOME SORT OF "EQUATORIAL" LINGO. IF **TEQUILA** WAS HERE I BET...

HEY! WAIT A MINUTE!!

"...THE JEWEL IN THE CHIEF'S SCEPTRE..."

"...IT'S EXACTLY LIKE THE ONE **MAX** STOLE FROM THE **IMPERIAL PALACE**"!!

"...THE EYE OF THE BLOATED TOAD"?...ARE YOU **SURE**?!!"

29

"IT CERTAINLY **LOOKS** THE SAME!"

"BUT I THOUGHT THE **EMPEROR** HAD THE LAST JEWEL BACK ON **HOMEWORLD!**"

"MAYBE HE JUST **THINKS** HE DOES, **LARRY**...OR MAYBE HE WANTS IT TO **LOOK** THAT WAY-- WHO **KNOWS!?!**"

"'WHO KNOWS?' HOW ABOUT 'WHO **CARES**'!! WE'VE GOT MORE IMPORTANT WOR-RIES, GUYS!!"

SUCH AS WHAT'S IN THIS **CAULDRON** THEY'RE BRINGING TOWARDS US!!

I DON'T KNOW...BUT I BET WE DON'T **LIKE** IT!!

PHAUGH!! "DON'T LIKE IT" IS RIGHT!!,.

THIS SWILL TASTES **HORRIBLE**!! LIKE,..BLEAH!.. TOADSTOOLS!

PROBABLY A HOMEBREW...

...TO MAKE THE SACRIFICIAL CEREMONY MORE...

GULP!!

"HANG ON GANG-- I HAVE A FEELING THIS COULD GET A LITTLE...WEIRD!!!"

"MAKE THAT VERY WEIRD!"

30

31

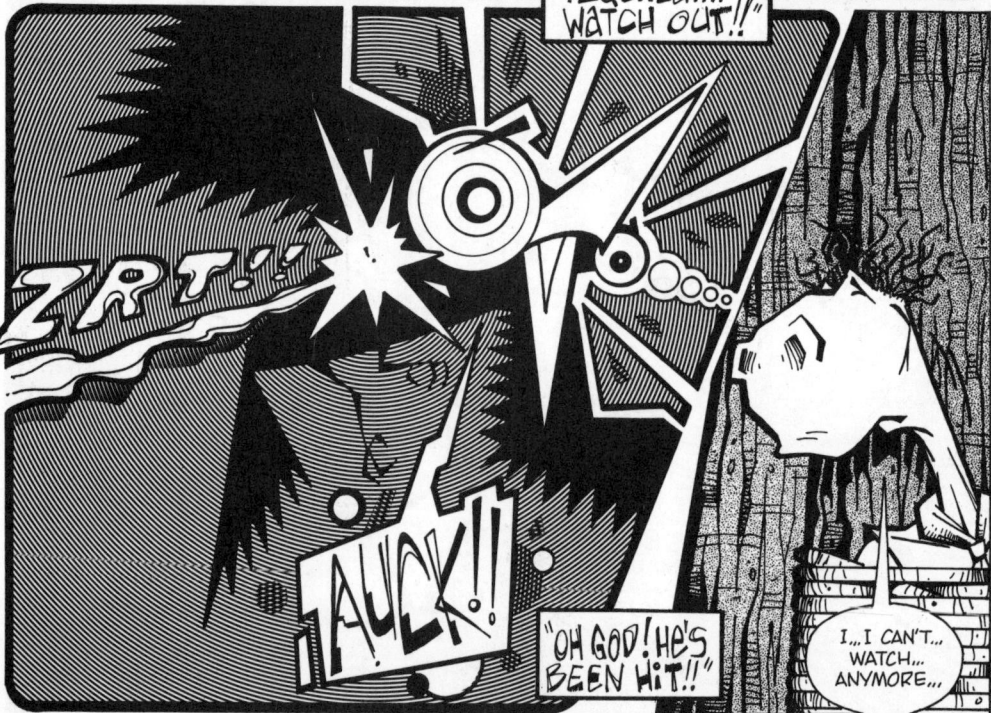

YOU ....DON'T.....UNDER.....STAND!!"

I'M...THE ONE WHO...DOESN'T UNDERSTAND! THE CHIEF... DROPPED THE KNIFE AND NOW HE'S BOWING AND SCRAPING LIKE SOME KIND OF FLUNKY!!

HEY KEVIN!! WHAT GIVES?!.. THESE BUSHTOADS COULDN'T WAIT TO CARVE THE THREE OF US UP...

BUT YOU!! YOU THEY'RE TREATING LIKE... LIKE THE EMPEROR FOR CHRISSAKE!

NOT THE EMPEROR, JERRY, BUT CLOSE!...

I'M HIS SON,

End of Chapter 4

IN THE IMPERIAL PALACE--ABOVE THE STREETS OF HOMEWORLD.

THE GUARDS FOUND HIM THIS MORNING, LORD GEKKUS...

...COLLAPSED NEAR HIS BED.

ONCE I KNEW HOW SERIOUS THE EMPEROR'S CONDITION WAS... I KNEW YOU WOULD WANT TO BE INFORMED!

I APPRECIATE THAT, DOCTOR.

HAS...HIS SON BEEN NOTIFIED?

PRINCE KEVIN IS STILL MISSING, SIR, BUT IF I MAY... I SUGGEST EFFORTS TO FIND HIM BE INTENSIFIED.

HIS HIGHNESS IS FIGHTING A GRIM BATTLE FOR HIS LIFE!

A BATTLE I FEAR HE IS LOSING.

IN SUCH CASES, A PATIENT'S WILL TO LIVE IS CRUCIAL.

KEVIN'S PRESENCE, AS MUCH AS ANYTHING, COULD VERY WELL SAVE THE EMPEROR'S LIFE!

I AM QUITE AWARE OF THAT, DOCTOR, AND REST ASSURED...

...NO ONE WANTS TO FIND THE PRINCE MORE THAN I.

35

SORRY I HAD TO LIE GUYS, BUT WHEN YOU BROKE INTO THE SPACESHIP BACK ON HOMEWORLD, I WAS READY TO BLAST OFF MYSELF!

I DIDN'T KNOW IF I COULD TRUST YOU THEN.

BUT KID... THAT STILL DOESN'T EXPLAIN WHY THE BUSHTOADS DIDN'T KILL YOU.

OH, I KNEW THEY WOULDN'T... NOT WHEN THEIR CHIEF SAW THIS AMULET.

MY FATHER GAVE IT TO ME WHEN HE EXPLAINED HOW HE BECAME EMPEROR.

"AFTER THE 'BLAST' OF '29, MY FATHER LED THE EXPEDITION TO ASSESS DAMAGE DONE TO THE MOON'S IRRIGATION PROJECT."

"HE FOUND THAT THE COMBINATION OF WATER AND NUCLEAR RADIATION HAD TRANSFORMED THE MOON INTO A TROPICAL JUNGLE -- TEEMING WITH MUTATED LIFE FORMS."

"THE BUSHTOADS?" "RIGHT, JERRY. THEY CALLED HIM 'THE SKY GOD' AND TOOK HIM TO THEIR TEMPLE... A TEMPLE OVERFLOWING WITH RADIOACTIVE GEMS."

"LIKE THE ONE THAT ZAPPED TEQUILA." "EXACTLY, MAX, THEY'RE AN UNLIMITED ENERGY SOURCE. MY FATHER TOOK ONE AND TOLD THE TOADS TO GUARD THE REST 'TIL HE CAME BACK."

WAIT A MINUTE!... ARE YOU SAYING THAT ONE JEWEL HAS KEPT THE GREAT MACHINES GOING ON HOMEWORLD FOR OVER FORTY YEARS?

NOT BAD, EH, JERRY? KEVIN'S FATHER SOLVES HOMEWORLD'S ENERGY CRISIS AND SETS UP A RELIGIOUS AND POLITICAL POWER BASE FOR HIMSELF TO BOOT!

IMPRESSIVE. BUT WHY'D YOU COME BACK FOR **MORE**?

MY **FATHER'S** A VERY **SICK MAN** AND HIS ASSISTANT, **LORD GEKKUS** CERTAINLY WILL **CONTEST** MY CLAIM TO THE THRONE SHOULD MY FATHER DIE.

BUT IF I GET TO THE JEWELS **FIRST**... THERE'S NO WAY HE CAN STOP ME FROM **TAKING OVER**!

COUNT US **IN**, KIDDO-- WE'LL BE HAPPY TO HELP YOU FIND THE **JEWELS**!

FOR A **PIECE** OF THE **ACTION**, OF COURSE. BUT WE'LL NEED **TEQUILA** TO **TRANSLATE**. IS HE FIXED YET?

LET'S TURN HIM ON AND WE'LL FIND OUT!

HMM... NEEDS A LITTLE FINE TUNING...

...AND HE'LL BE GOOD AS NEW.

¡¡**DIOS MIO**!! THAT WAS **CLOSE**! THOSE **ESTUPID TOADS** ALMOST **FRICASSEED** ME FOR GOOD! **DEAD**!! ¡¡**MUERTO**!!!!

EASY, TK! **EASY**! WE DIDN'T PUT YOU BACK TOGETHER TO **BABBLE**...WE NEED YOU TO TALK TO THE CHIEF!

ASK HIM IF HE CAN LEAD US TO THE JEWELS.

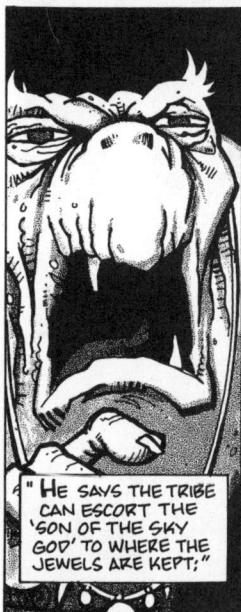

" **HE** SAYS THE TRIBE CAN ESCORT THE 'SON OF THE SKY GOD' TO WHERE THE JEWELS ARE KEPT;"

"...**AT** THE TEMPLE OF THE **BLOATED TOAD**!"

BOY, LIMITLESS WEALTH, AN INFINITE ENERGY SOURCE, AND A POLITICAL TAKE OVER!

THIS OPERATION'S FINALLY STARTING TO COME TOGETHER!

DIDN'T I TELL YOU TO HAVE A LITTLE FAITH, LARRY?

WITH OUR CUT OF THE TREASURE, WE'LL HAVE HOMEWORLD DANCING TO OUR TUNE FOR A CHANGE!

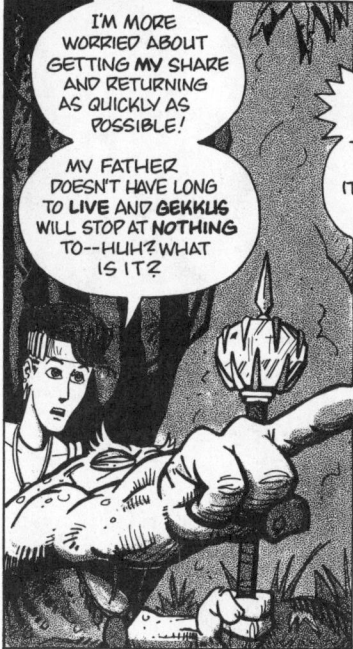

I'M MORE WORRIED ABOUT GETTING MY SHARE AND RETURNING AS QUICKLY AS POSSIBLE!

MY FATHER DOESN'T HAVE LONG TO LIVE AND GEKKUS WILL STOP AT NOTHING TO--HUH? WHAT IS IT?

ALL..RIGHT!.

THE TOADS CAME THROUGH FOR US! IT'S THE ENTRANCE TO THE SACRED TEMPLE!

HMPH!. IT'S SEEN BETTER DAYS!

HAVEN'T WE ALL!

THE ENTRANCE IS BLOCKED, BUT ⹂OOF⹂ I...THINK I CAN ⹂ACK⹂ GET TH...

...ROOOOOOOOO

CRASH!

JEEZ, MAX!. YOU OK?

UH, YEAH... I GUESS...JUST A LITTLE SHOOK UP. I...

HOLY HAT!! HEY GUYS!! GET DOWN HERE QUICK!..

39

THE CRASH SITE, SIR... NO REMAINS... NO SIGNS OF LIFE. EVERYTHING HAS BEEN VIRTUALLY PULVERIZED. BEYOND RECOGNITION.

I'M POSITIVE WE CAN REPORT TO LORD GEKKUS THAT THE ALLEGED THIEVES WERE KILLED UPON IMPACT!

THE CHANCES OF SURVIVING SUCH A FALL ARE APPROXIMATELY 1,475,000:1.

DO NOT SEEK TO IMPRESS ME VIT STATISTICS, SARGEANT...

DER HOLO BROTHERS HAFF ELUDED ME BEFORE, BY BEATING GREATER ODDS THAN THAT!

SCOUT DER AREA... IF THEY ARE ALIVE—I VILL FIND THEM. UND IF I FIND THEM...

...THEY VILL NOT BE ALIVE FOR LONG!!

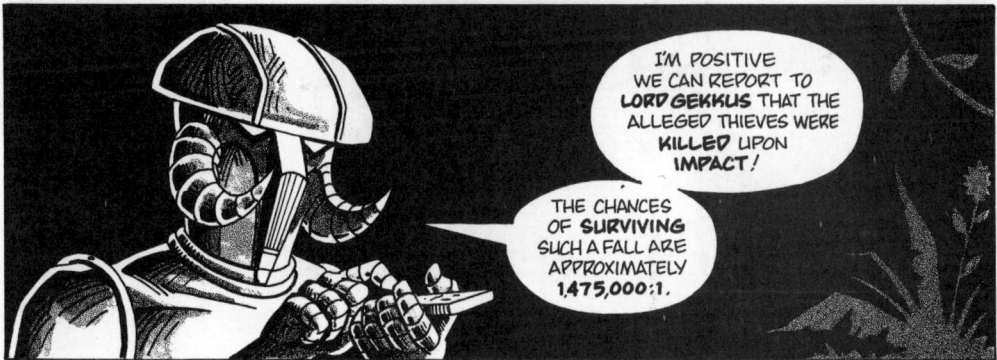

End of Chapter 5

TWO A.M.: HOMEWORLD. IN THE DARK, EMPTY HALLS OF THE **IMPERIAL PALACE**, **LORD GEKKUS** ENTERS THE EMPEROR'S **MEDICAL CHAMBERS**.

AND SO YOU STRUGGLE **ON**, EH, OLD MAN?

CLINGING HOPELESSLY TO LIFE EVEN AS THIS DISEASE **FURTHER** RAVAGES YOU.

IRONIC, ISN'T IT! THAT **YOU**,...HAVING EXPLOITED THE FAITH AND SUPERSTITION OF **SO MANY** NOW FALL PREY TO YOUR **OWN** DARKEST FEARS.

YOUR DOCTORS CAN NOT HELP YOU **THIS TIME**, CAN THEY, "YOUR HIGHNESS"? THE **CAUSE** OF YOUR ILLNESS IS **UNKNOWN** TO THEM. HOW COULD THEY **BEGIN** TO GUESS WHAT **WE BOTH** KNOW TO BE **TRUE**.

THAT IT IS THE **CURSE** WHICH WEAKENS YOU,...

THE CURSE OF THE **TEMPLE** YOU **VIOLATED** YEARS AGO...

THE **CURSE** OF THE **BLOATED TOAD**!!

42

YOU SEE SERGEANT? DER HOLO BROTHERS **HAFF** SURVIVED, **DESPITE** YOUR PREVIOUS CALCULATIONS. DER TRAIL FROM DER **CRASH SITE** LEADS **DIRECTLY** TO THIS CLEARING.

UND THESE PREHISTORIC ARTIFACTS SUGGEST DER MOON IS NOT AS UNINHABITED AS ONCE THOUGHT.

YES, **HERR LIPPMAN**, THIS ALTAR AND THOSE POSTS MUST MEAN THE THIEVES WERE PART OF A PRIMITIVE SACRIFICIAL CEREMONY.

SURELY, THEY DIDN'T SURVIVE **THAT** AS WELL.

DO NOT ASSUME **ANYTHING** WHEN DEALING VIT DER **HOLO** BROTHERS. THEY HAFF AN **IRRITATING** HABIT OF **SURVIVING** ALL **SORTS** OF DILEMMAS...

...A HABIT I'LL **RID** THEM OF, SHOULD WE MEET AGAIN.

EITHER WAY, I MUST BE COMPLETELY **CERTAIN** BEFORE I REPORT BACK TO **LORD GEKKUS**...

...TOLERANCE FOR AMBIGUITY IS NOT ONE OF HIS BETTER TRAITS.

OF COURSE, SERGEANT, IF YOU WOULD LIKE TO TELL HIM YOURSELF... WELL, WELL.

IT APPEARS OUR **PERSISTENCE** HAS **PAID** OFF, GENTLEMEN.

A TEMPLE OF SORTS...UND **LAUGHTER**...FROM WITHIN.

COMRADES... I BELIEVE OUR SEARCH HAS **ENDED**.

43

The HOLO. Brothers in CROSSFIRE!

I HAVE TO **HAND** IT TO YOU, **MAX**,,, WE'VE CERTAINLY HIT THE JACKPOT **THIS** TIME!

AND THANKS TO **KEVIN**, THIS **BUSHTOAD TEMPLE** WITH ALL ITS JEWELS IS **OURS** FOR THE **TAKING**! ALL WE...

JEEZUS JERRY,,, TRY 'N' SHOW A LITTLE **RESTRAINT**, OK?

hee hee,,, I CAN'T **HELP** IT, **MAX**,,, hee hee,,, WE'RE RICH!,,, hee hee,,, AND I'M SO **HAPPY!** hee hee hee

JIM RYAN
SCRIPT & ART
GARY FIELDS LETTERS

PSST!,, **LARRY**!,, IS, UH, **JERRY** ALWAYS THIS UNINHIBITED? I MEAN, FIRST HE'S CHASING WOMEN THROUGH MARSHES, AND NOW,,,

HAH!! YOU THINK THIS IS BAD?,,

",,WAIT UNTIL YOU'VE SEEN HIM **EAT**!"

MONEY MONEY MONEY MONEY MONEY!!

SI, JERRY ALWAYS DID GO FOR THE MORE EARTHIER THINGS IN LIFE...

COME HERE, FELLAS, THIS LOOKS MUY INTERESANTE.

"IT'S HIEROGLYPHICS ESPLAINING THE EMPEROR'S VISIT AND HOW THE BUSHTOADS PLEDGED FEALTY TO HIM AND HIS OFFSPRING."

JUST LIKE I SAID: THE BUSHTOADS WILL DO ANYTHING I SAY BECAUSE I'M SORT OF A GOD TO THEM.

YOU? A GOD? THAT'S A LAUGH! THESE TOADS ARE ABOUT AS GULLIBLE AS YOU CAN GET!!

NO MORE GULLIBLE THAN THE PEOPLE OF HOMEWORLD, JERRY. REMEMBER: THE EMPEROR HAS THEM BELIEVING THE DIAMONDS ARE SACRED GEMS...

...WHEN THEY'RE JUST RADIOACTIVE FUEL FOR THE GREAT MACHINES.

USING A BOGUS RELIGION TO KEEP THE POPULATION IN LINE, EH? YOU GOTTA LOVE IT.

HEY,... I APPRECIATE A GOOD SCAM AS MUCH AS THE NEXT GUY, JERRY, BUT LET'S GET THESE LAST JEWELS OUTTA HERE! OK?..

..I DON'T WANT TO OVERSTAY OUR ☼

...WELCOME.

THINK FAST, HOLOGRAM!!

THINK FAST,...OR DIE!!

45

46

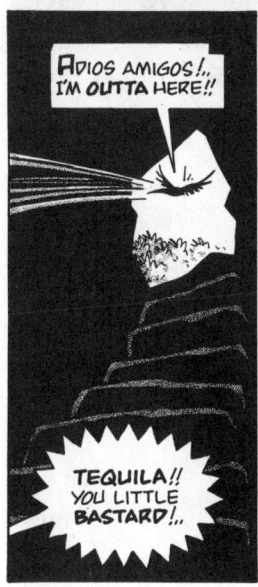

47

YOU ALWAYS **WERE** A SWEET TALKER, **FRANZ**...

"...BUT I THINK WE'LL PASS!"

ZZTTT!!

PING!

I'LL DRAW THIER FIRE, **MAX!** YOU TAKE CARE OF **LIPPMAN!!**

THAT'S THE LAST OF **YOUR** MEN!..

...IT'S JUST YOU'N ME NOW, CATMAN!

LOOK LARRY, THE IDOL!!..

48

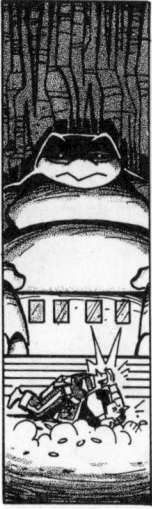

"IT'S... STARTING... TO... MOVE!!"

End of Chapter 6

49

The HOLD Brothers IN IDOL THREATS!

HANG ON, **MAX**! A COUPLE A' **SHOTS** FROM THIS **BLASTER**...

"...OUGHT TO CHANGE HIS MIND **REAL** FAST!"

RRRR?..

"UH... THEN AGAIN..."

...MAYBE N- ARGGH!!

THAK!

WELL, SO MUCH FOR USING **BLASTERS** ON HIM!

YOU OK, **JERRY** ?

I DON'T BELIEVE IT, **LARRY**!.. WE FINALLY HIT THE **JACK-POT**!-- **MILLIONS** OF **JEWELS** AND **DIAMONDS** IN THIS CAVE AND WE CAN'T GET THEM OUT 'CAUSE SOME **FREAKIN' IDOL'S** ON THE **WARPATH**!!

"**CASHING** IN OUR LOOT'S THE **LEAST** OF OUR PROBLEMS, **JERRY**,..."

"THAT IDOL'S NOT THINKING ABOUT **MONEY**..."

"HE'S THINKING ABOUT DINNER!"

CRUNCH MUNCH CHOMP!

GOTT IN HIMMEL!!

TO THINK THAT THE BUSHTOADS USED TO WORSHIP THAT THING. SO MUCH FOR DIVINE GRATITUDE!!

IF WE DON'T THINK OF SOMETHING QUICK!..

I THINK WE'RE GONNA BE THE MAIN COURSE!

MEANWHILE...

¿SO LOS HOLOS THOUGHT I DITCHED 'EM, EH? THEY SHOULD KNOW BETTER!

I JUS' KNEW WE'D NEED A WAY TO GET THE JEWELS BACK TO HOMEWORLD.

AN' AS THE SAYING GOES, "WHERE THERE'S A 'LIPPMAN'..."

"...THERE'S AN ESPACE CRUISER!!"

"AND IN ORDER TO GET THE SHIP..."

¡YOU TAKE OUT THE GUARD!!

THWOK!!

THEN ENTER THE COCK PIT...

HOOK UP THE PILOT COMPUTER...

..... HOPE YOUR FEET REACH THE PEDAL....

AND TAKE OFF!!

LES' JUS' HOPE THE BOYS ARE ESTILL IN ONE PIECE WHEN I GET THERE!

SSHOOOOO......

THIS IS GROTESQUE!! THOSE POOR TOADS DON'T STAND A CHANCE! CAN'T WE DO ANY-THING, LARRY?

I'M OPEN TO SUGGES-TIONS, KEVIN. WITHOUT MORE FIREPOWER WE...

MUNCH! MUNCH! GULP!

THE CHIEF'S SCEPTRE! THERE SHOULD BE ENOUGH ENERGY IN THAT TO MAKE THE IDOL THINK TWICE!!

GOOD IDEA. COVER ME.

NO, KEVIN. I'M SICK OF SIT-TING ON THE SIDELINES!

YOU COVER ME!!

"COME BACK, LARRY,...HE SEES YOU!!"

LOOKS LIKE...≷OW≷ THE IDOL'S SICK OF...≷URG≷ TOAD MUNCHIES...

...AND ACQUIRED... ≷UNGH≷ A TASTE FOR...≷OOF≷ HOLO-GRAM TIDBITS!!

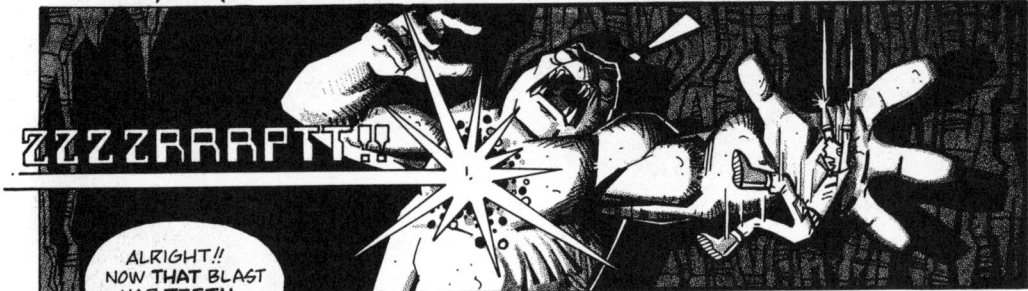

ZZZZRRRPTT!!

ALRIGHT!! NOW THAT BLAST HAD TEETH IN IT!!

BUT WHO... Z

IT CAME FROM OUT HERE. HAH! I DON'T BELIEVE IT!..

"...IT'S TEQUILA!.. WITH A STAR CRUISER!!"

HOP IN, CABALLEROS!..

...THE FLYING ES FINE!

nein!!!..

YOU GOT THE JEWELS, MAX?

JUST THESE TWO--THE REST ARE BURIED WITH THE IDOL AND LIPPMAN.

RMBLR RMBRK KKRRASH!

LIPPMAN? ≷PHEW!!≷ WHATTA WAY TA GO!!

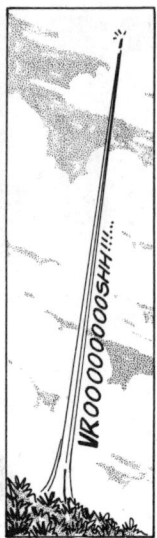

VROOOOOOOOSHH!!......

"YEAH, I'M 'HEART-BROKEN!'"

"YOU CRACKED THE CODE YET, T.K.?"

"SI, WE'LL BE ABLE TO LAND ON HOMEWORLD NOW, NO PROBLEM."

"SNIFF."

"WHAT'S WRONG, JERRY?"

ALL THOSE JEWELS... ≷SNIFF≷ GONE!!

DON'T PUSH IT, PAL! WE'RE ALIVE, AREN'T WE?

BESIDES, TWO ARE ALL WE REALLY NEED-- ONE TO CASH IN AND ONE TO FUEL THE GREAT MACHINES.

...AND DON'T FORGET MY FATHER'S GRATITUDE-- THIS JEWEL WILL KEEP HIS ADMINISTRATION SECURE...

...AND I'M SURE I CAN SWING SOME "CUSH" GOVERNMENT JOBS FOR YOU!

"US!?...G-MEN? HAH!! WELL WHADDAYA KNOW!"

"LOOKS LIKE EVERYTHING'S GOING TO WORK OUT AFTER ALL."

56

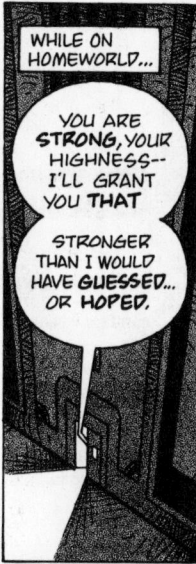

Imperial MEMO

TO – LORD GEKKUS – Senior Administrator of Religious Propaganda and Interplanetary Relations.

REGARDING – Update on "Eye of the Bloated Toad" jewel theft and consequent rise in revolutionary activity.

SUSPECTS –

The HOLO. Brothers

BACKGROUND – Raised in orphanage, parents unknown. History at orphanage and state reform school one of anarchy and insubordination.

Nickname "Hologram Brothers" refers to non-existent status conferred upon them by school officials. Trio separated when leader, Max, was thrown in jail during street riots.

Maxwell HOLOGRAM

Served 2 years in regional penitentiary for "assault with intent to throttle".

Upon release became part of an urban underground dealing with contraband, fallen women and state-banned music.

Intelligence and "street smarts" overshadowed by a total lack of morals and cynical view of social responsibility.

Jerome
HOLOGRAM

Enlisted in Imperial "Perimeter Squad" — trained in ancient warfare techniques. 3-year AWOL charge dropped after supplying information to local authorities about narcotic trade routes on Anthrax XI.

A historian, soldier, debaucher — alarmingly dedicated to conspicuous consumption.

He is cheerful by nature, but the most dangerous of the group once provoked.

Lawrence
HOLOGRAM

6 years training in Artificial Intelligence, Military Cybernetics and Political Philosophy.

Linked with infamous "Optical Fiber Wars" of '28. 5 indictments, no convictions.

Warning — Quiet demeanor should not be misinterpreted — while not as physically inclined as his partners, his intelligence and technical background make him potentially the most threatening.

Tequila
MOCKING BIRD

Missing — One (1) Communications and Data Analysis Android — Mockingbird series, #TK58. Believed stolen/escaped from RoboCorp. Mechanical error when assembled believed responsible for rebellious nature and unstable emotional make-up.

CONCLUSION —

The combination of the HOLO. Brothers diverse talents and Tequila Mockingbird facility with information retrieval and military tactics present a tangible threat to this administration's political solvency.

Terminate — They are dangerous and certifiably insane.

HERE'S THE LOWDOWN SO FAR: THE **HOLO. BROTHERS**, THREE MAKE-SHIFT MERCENARIES, HAVE RETURNED TO **HOMEWORLD** FROM THE BUSH TOAD PLANET WITH THE **SACRED GEMS**, USED TO FUEL THE **GREAT MACHINES**........,THE **HOLOS.**, ALONG WITH **TEQUILA MOCKING-BIRD** ARE ALSO HELPING **PRINCE KEVIN** TAKE HIS RIGHTFUL PLACE AS LEADER OF THE EMPIRE, DUE TO THE DEATH OF HIS FATHER, THE EMPEROR. SO IF YOU'RE READY...LETS JOIN

The HOLO. Brothers IN street scam

THREAT!

JEEZ MAX, THESE STREETS ARE *DEAD!* WHERE THE HELL IS EVERYONE ?

I DON'T KNOW, AND I DON'T *CARE,* **JERRY**...

...*CONSIDERING* OUR "STATUS" WITH THE FEDS, THE FEWER PEOPLE WE MEET, THE BETTER!

TRUE ENOUGH! MY ONLY CHANCE OF ASSUMING POWER IS GETTING INSIDE THE PALACE SOON-- BEFORE **GEKKUS** TAKES OVER COMPLETELY.

THAT MAY NOT BE SO EASY, KEVIN !!

LOOK!!

JIM ROHN
SCRIPT & ART
GARY FIELDS
LETTERS

A NEWS CONFERENCE. NO WONDER THE STREETS ARE EMPTY.

SI, NO ONE MISSES ONE OF THEM.

"AND THERE'S **GEKKUS** ADDRESSING THE CROWD!"

PEOPLE OF HOME-WORLD... I HAVE NEW INFORMATION CONCERNING THE EMPEROR'S DEATH AND THE THEFT OF THE HOLY GEM THAT RE-QUIRES YOUR IMMEDIATE ACTION...

WE HAVE LEARNED THAT OUR LEADER DID **NOT** DIE OF THE ILLNESS WHICH LONG PLAGUED HIM, BUT WAS **MURDERED**, MUR-DERED IN COLD BLOOD!!.. ...AND THE MURDERER'S THREE ACCOMPLICES ARE THE **CHIEF SUSPECTS** IN THE HOLY GEM ROBBERY.

MAX HOLOGRAM – EX CON AND BLACK MARKET RACKETEER.

JEROME HOLOGRAM – FORMER A.W.O.L. SOLDIER WITH THE PERIMETER SQUAD.

LAWRENCE HOLOGRAM – SUB-VERSIVE ACTIVIST IN OPTIC FIBER REBELLION OF '28.

THESE THREE ARE WANTED FOR HELPING **PRINCE KEVIN** -- HEIR APPARENT TO THE THRONE OF **HOMEWORLD**.

ME!?! WHAT'S **GEKKUS** TRYING TO PULL HERE?

I DON'T KNOW, BUT I BET WE DON'T LIKE IT!!

62

YES, **PRINCE KEVIN**, THE EMPEROR'S ONLY SON... I SPOKE OF SHOCK EARLIER, MY FRIENDS, AND NO DETAIL OF THE EMPEROR'S DEATH IS **MORE** SHOCKING THAN THE FACT THAT THE PRINCE WAS THE LAST PERSON TO SEE HIS FATHER ALIVE.

BUT BECAUSE OF JEALOUSY, LUST FOR POWER AND OTHER MOTIVES I CAN SCARCELY GUESS AT, HIS VISIT TO HIS FATHER'S HOSPITAL SUITE WAS **NOT** THAT OF A LOVING SON...

...**NOT** THAT OF A CONCERNED SUBJECT, BUT OF A **KILLER**, AN ASSASSIN!!...

...FOR **PRINCE KEVIN** HAS MURDERED THE EMPEROR!!..

...HE HAS KILLED HIS OWN FATHER!!

I KILLED HIM!?! WHY THAT LYING, SCHEMING...

SHHH-- KEEP IT DOWN, **KEVIN**,... IF THE GUARDS RECOGNIZE YOU...

"..WE'RE DONE FOR..."

"KEVIN,"

"KEVIN"?

KEVIN! IT'S THE PRINCE!

DEATH TO THE PRINCE!!...

DEATH TO THE TRAITORS!! !!!!

63

THE HOLY GEM IS GONE... THE EMPEROR IS GONE... OUR PRINCE-- A WANTED CRIMINAL...

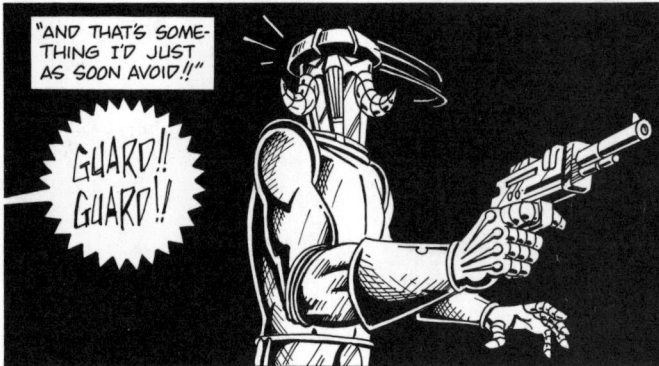

THE FUTURE LOOKS **BLEAK,** BUT I BELIEVE HOMEWORLD WILL SURVIVE THIS **DARK DAY.**

REST ASSURED, THE EMPIRE **WILL** BE RESTORED TO ITS FORMER **GLORY!**

AND... SHOULD THE PEOPLE OF HOMEWORLD, WHEN **CHOOSING** THEIR NEXT EMPEROR... FEEL THAT I ,...

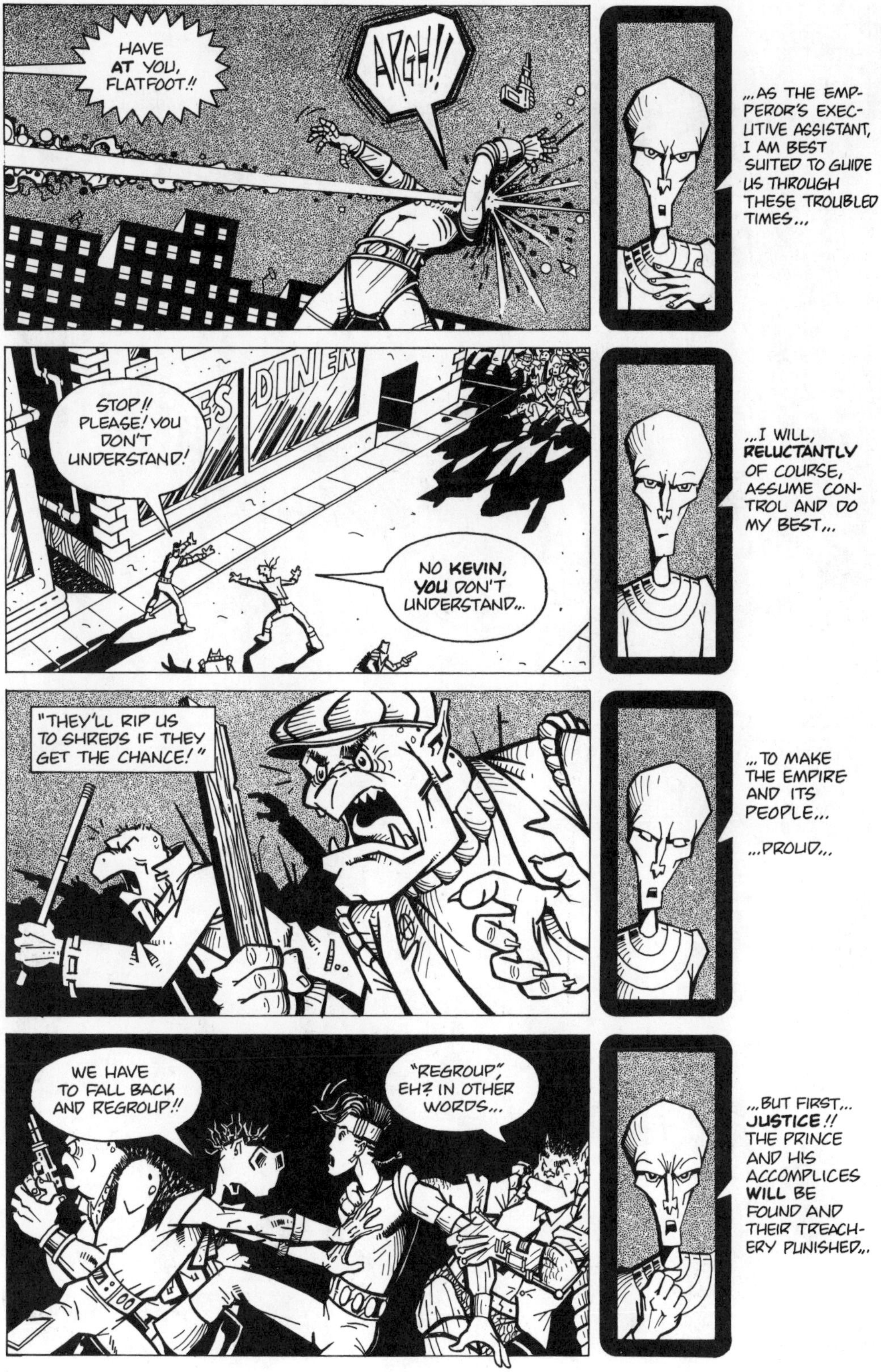
HAVE AT YOU, FLATFOOT!!
ARGH!!
...AS THE EMPEROR'S EXECUTIVE ASSISTANT, I AM BEST SUITED TO GUIDE US THROUGH THESE TROUBLED TIMES...
DINER
STOP!! PLEASE! YOU DON'T UNDERSTAND!
NO KEVIN, YOU DON'T UNDERSTAND...
...I WILL, RELUCTANTLY OF COURSE, ASSUME CONTROL AND DO MY BEST...
"THEY'LL RIP US TO SHREDS IF THEY GET THE CHANCE!"
...TO MAKE THE EMPIRE AND ITS PEOPLE...
...PROUD...
WE HAVE TO FALL BACK AND REGROUP!!
"REGROUP", EH? IN OTHER WORDS...
...BUT FIRST... JUSTICE!! THE PRINCE AND HIS ACCOMPLICES WILL BE FOUND AND THEIR TREACHERY PUNISHED...

End of Chapter 8

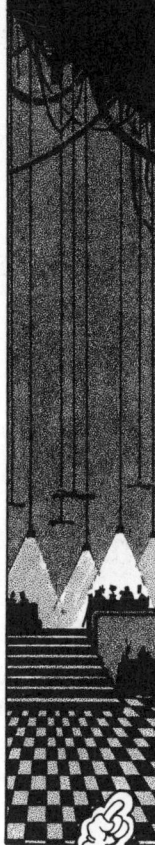

GUYS, I'D LIKE YOU TO MEET **ETHEL PENTAGRAM**-- OWNER OF THE INDIGO LOUNGE...

...AND PRETTIEST FENCE AMONG THE "UPPER CRUST"!

HI FELLAS, T'SUP?

I HAVE THE PLANS RIGHT HERE...COST ME **PLENTY**, **MAX**, I PULLED A LOT OF **STRINGS!**

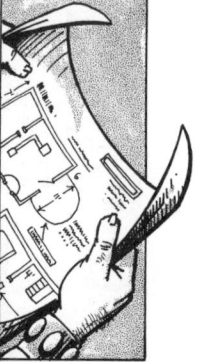

"DON'T **WORRY**, KID, THIS IS BIG--**REAL** BIG AND YOU'RE IN FOR A PIECE OF THE **ACTION!**"

"**HMPH!** I'VE HEARD **THAT** BEFORE! HEY, HOW ABOUT SITTIN' IN WITH THE **BAND, MAX?** THE GUYS SAY **NO ONE** SINGS "LITTLE RED ROOSTER" BETTER THAN **YOU!**"

"I'LL HAVE TO PASS, PENNY. LOW PROFILE, Y'KNOW?"

HMMM... I WAS **WONDERING** WHAT THE **SHADES** WERE FOR!... WELL, SEE YOU GUYS AROUND OK?

WHAT A GAL. A REAL ROCK!

WHAT'S WITH **YOU,** JERRY?

HAH! I WAS JUST THINKIN'... WE SHOULD MAKE **T.K.** AND THE KID HONORARY **HOLO BROTHERS!**

THEY'VE BEEN **ACES** THROUGH THIS THIS WHOLE "HOLY GEM" GIG.

US? HOLO BROTHERS? BUT WE'RE NOT EVEN RELATED!

IT DOESN'T MATTER, **KEVIN**...IT'S JUST A NICKNAME WE GOT GROWING UP IN THE ORPHANAGE.

WHAT DO YOU SAY TO **THAT?**

I SAY: HERE'S TO THE FIVE HOLO BROTHERS!

A QUINTET OF MACHISMO!

70

THE **HOLO BRO-THERS** AND 'PRINCE KEVIN' HAVE LEFT THE BAR, M'LORD.

WITH THE **BLUE PRINTS?**

YES, SIR.

...AND HEADING FOR THE IMPERIAL PALACE WITH GRAND THOUGHTS OF **CONQUEST**, NO DOUBT.

THE **PALACE**, SIRE?

THE **PALACE**, MS. PENTAGRAM, WHERE THE **HOLO BROTHERS** OBVIOUSLY PLAN TO BARGE IN ON "GEKKUS'" CORONATION AND FOIL HIS ASCENT TO POWER.

SUCH **ARROGANCE!**.. TO THINK THAT **THEY**, AS THE EMPIRE'S SAVIORS, COULD CHANGE ITS FATE SO EASILY.

NO, THEY ARE IN FACT, MERE **PAWNS** IN A GAME FOR CONTROL OF THE ENTIRE **EMPIRE**.

AND IN SUCH GAMES IT IS RARELY THE **PAWNS** THAT SURVIVE!

End of Chapter 9

71

"THERE IT IS, KIDS-- THE IMPERIAL PALACE!"

"AND GEKKUS IS INSIDE PREPARING FOR THE CORONATION CEREMONY EVEN AS WE SPEAK."

ANY IDEAS ON GETTING IN THERE, MAX?

WELL WE CAN'T JUST WALK IN--THEY'LL BE CHECKING ALL I.D.'S AND WE'RE PRETTY HOT PROPERTY RIGHT NOW.

SI, MUY CALIENTE!

THAT'S WHAT THESE PLANS ARE FOR--OUR BEST BET IS TO USE THE SEWERS, GO THROUGH THE BACK CORRIDORS OF THE PALACE AND INTO THE SERVANT'S QUARTERS.

THE SEWERS, EH? HMMPH!! NOTHING LIKE GOING "IN STYLE"!

SHHH!! YOU TRYING TO BRING THE GUARDS?

CLICK CHICK

ARE YOU KIDDING, LARRY?.. EVEN THE RATS DON'T MAKE IT THIS FAR DOWN.!

SI.!! I THIN' I KNOW WHY...THE SMELL IS MUY HEDIONDO!

C'MON LET'S SEE IF WE CAN FIND ANYTHING IN-TERESTING.

CLANG!!

REGARDING HERR LIPPMAN, SIR, THE SECOND SCOUTING PARTY FOUND NO SURVIVORS.

NO SURVIVORSZ.. HOW ODD.

I WOULD HAVE THOUGHT LIPPMAN TO BE MORE... RESILIENT THAN THAT.

THOSE THIEVES HE WAS PURSUING-- WHAT WERE THEIR NAMES AGAINZ

THE "HOLO" BROTHERS, I BELIEVE.

YES, YES. I AM MORE CONVINCED THAN EVER THAT THESE "HOLO BROTHERS" HAVE ALLIED THEMSELVES WITH PRINCE KEVIN IN AN EFFORT TO DISRUPT THE CEREMONY TONIGHT.

BUT I'LL NOT ALLOW THEIR JUVENILE ACTIONS FOIL MY PLANS.

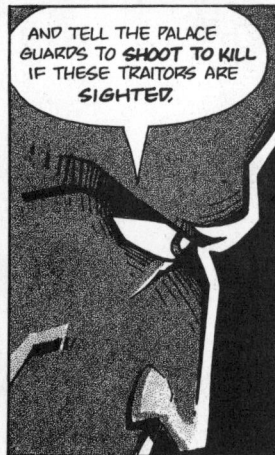

INCREASE SECURITY AT ALL ENTRANCES AND DOUBLE-CHECK THE INVITATIONS OF ALL GUESTS.

AND TELL THE PALACE GUARDS TO SHOOT TO KILL IF THESE TRAITORS ARE SIGHTED.

"DID YOU SAY 'INTERESTING,' MAX? HOW 'BOUT REMARKABLE! THIS MUST BE THE BASE OF ONE OF THE GREAT MACHINES... THE CENTER OF POWER FOR ALL OF HOMEWORLD!"

♪O ESTAIRS!!. GUESS I'LL SEE YOU GUYS AT THE TOP, AMIGOS!

HMM... IT'S STILL HUMMING... GEKKUS MUST HAVE THE HOLY GEM LIPPMAN STOLE FROM US AT THE STRIPED APE.

BUT... BY THE TIME HE DIED HE COULD BARELY KEEP HOMEWORLD'S POLITICS UNDER CONTROL.

IT'S FUNNY THO-- HE KNEW THERE WERE MORE BACK ON THE MOON -- BUT HE WOULDN'T GO BACK-- USED TO TALK ABOUT THE TEMPLE BEING HAUNTED... AND THE DANGER IN ABUSING THE GEM'S POWER.

I ALWAYS THOUGHT IT WAS THE ILLNESS BEHIND THE BABBLING, BUT...

NO WONDER HE'S PLANNING ON TAKING OVER. HE THINKS HE HAS THE ONLY ONE.

BUT WE GOT THIS BABY-- AND WE KNOW WHERE THERE'S MORE ON THE MOON.

MY FATHER TOLD ME THAT AT ONE TIME THE WHOLE GALAXY WAS POWERED BY STONES LIKE THESE.

FREAKIN' FOUR HUNDRED STORIES.

YEAH, BUT MAYBE HE RAN INTO THE BUSH TOAD IDOL JUST LIKE WE DID.

75

TWENTY YEARS.

FOR **TWENTY YEARS** I'VE WATCHED AS THE "LATE" EMPEROR **SUCCEEDED** IN CONVINCING THE PEOPLE OF **HOMEWORLD** THAT THE **DIAMONDS** USED TO FUEL THE **GREAT MACHINES** WERE **HOLY GEMS.**

RELIGIOUS **ARTIFACTS** RATHER THAN MERE **RADIO-ACTIVE STONES.**

TWENTY YEARS... AND AS THE RELIGIOUS **POWER** GREW, SO DID THE EMPEROR'S **CLAIM** TO THE **THRONE...** FOR HE HAD **SUCCEEDED** IN FOREVER LINKING HIS **FORTUNES** TO THE **RELIGIOUS CONVICTIONS** OF HIS **SUBJECTS.**

A **PARTNER-SHIP** OF **SUPERSTITION** AND POLITICAL **NECESSITY** THAT I **ALSO** SHALL CONTINUE AS LONG AS IT **SERVES** MY PURPOSE.

BUT WHEREAS THE **EMPEROR**, IN HIS DECLINING YEARS, BEGAN TO ACTUALLY **BELIEVE** IN THE DIVINE NATURE OF THE GEMS AND THEIR SUPPOSED **"CURSE"** IF MISUSED, I WILL REFUSE TO SUCCUMB TO SUCH RELIGIOUS **PRATTLE.**

AND SHOULD THAT ROYAL **BRAT** AND HIS BAND OF **CRETINS...**

...TRY TO **INTERFERE** WITH MY WELL-LAID **PLANS...**

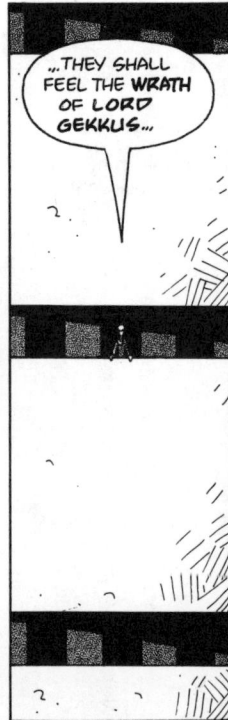

...THEY SHALL FEEL THE **WRATH** OF **LORD GEKKUS...**

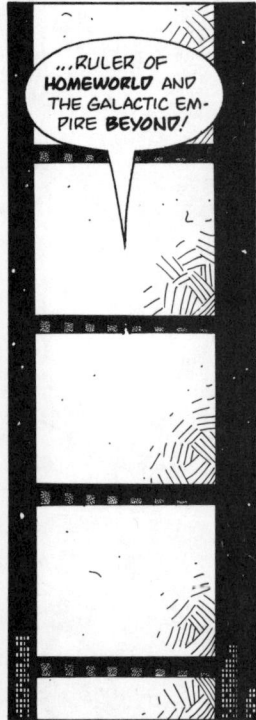

...RULER OF **HOMEWORLD** AND THE GALACTIC EMPIRE **BEYOND!**

76

End of Chapter 10

The H.O.L.D. Brothers in BALLROOM BLITZ!!

IT IS *CORONATION NIGHT* ON HOMEWORLD.

AND AS A *STORM* BREWS OUTSIDE, PROVIDING AN *OMINOUS* COUNTER-POINT TO THE FESTIVITIES *WITHIN...*

...THE CITY'S *ELITE* MEET TO CELEBRATE *LORD GEKKUS'* ASCENSION TO POWER.

MY FRIENDS...

TONIGHT IS A NIGHT OF *CELEBRATION*-- FOR *MYSELF,* OF COURSE, BUT ALSO FOR *YOU*-- THE *PEOPLE* OF HOMEWORLD.

YOU HAVE *SUFFERED* UNDER THE *DIM,DYING* REIGN OF THE *EMPEROR,* YOU HAVE *ENDURED* THE *BETRAYAL* OF HIS SON, AND YOU HAVE BEEN FORCED TO WATCH *HOME-WORLD'S* GLORY WITHER AWAY--ATROPHY TO THE VERY *BRINK* OF EXTINCTION.

TOO *LONG,* MY FRIENDS-- YOU HAVE WAITED *FAR* TOO LONG!

WITH THE ADVENT OF MY *CORONATION,* I PROMISE A *FRESH START*-- A CHANCE TO RECLAIM THE *GREATNESS* THAT WAS ONCE *YOURS* .

AND... I ALSO PROMISE YOU A *NIGHT* YOU WILL NOT SOON *FORGET!*

JIM BALENT SCRIPT 'N' ART
GARY FIELDS LETTERING

78

CLAP CLAP CLAP clap

I'LL GIVE HIM A NIGHT HE WON'T **FORGET!**

LOOK AT HIM, GUYS--**MILKIN'** THIS THING FOR ALL ITS **WORTH!** WHAT A **HAM**!!...

...WELL, HE'S IN FOR A **BIG** SURPRISE ONCE WE PUT **YOUR** PLAN INTO **ACTION**, RIGHT, MAX₹

MY PLAN₹

YEAH, **YOUR** PLAN! YOU KNOW-- THE WAY WE'RE GONNA STOP THIS CORONATION₹

HELL, I DON'T KNOW HOW! I'M PLAYIN' ALL THIS BY EAR, JERRY!

LET'S SEE... MAYBE START A **COMMOTION** AND SEE WHAT **HAPPENS** I **GUESS.**

YOU GUESS!₹! YOU GUESS!₹!

YOU'RE JUST **WINGING** IT, AREN'T YOU, MAX₹ **TYPICAL.** JUST **TYPICAL!**

¡**O**H MAN-- WE'RE GON' GET KEELED AN' YOU DON' E'EN HAFF A **PLAN!**

"WHAT ARE YOU GUYS **BITCHIN'** ABOUT₹ I GOT YOU **UP** HERE, DIDN'T I₹ **YOU** THINK UP THE REST **YOURSELF!!"**

SHHHH! TAKE IT **EASY**, GUYS! I HAVE A COUPLE OF IDEAS.

YOU!!

THO **THERE** YOU ARE, YOU THLACKERTH! FILL UP WATER ON TABLE **THIX** AND **YOU** THREE THEE IF THE **THERVITH BAR** NEEDTH YOU!

HUP! HUP! **PUSH DRINKTH!** PUSH **DRINKTH!**

79

YOU RAT BASTARD! KNOCKIN' OFF A KID JUST TO TAKE OVER, EH?!

THOK!

WELL, I DON'T LIKE IT!!

NOT... ONE... BIT!!

ZZZZ!!

TING!

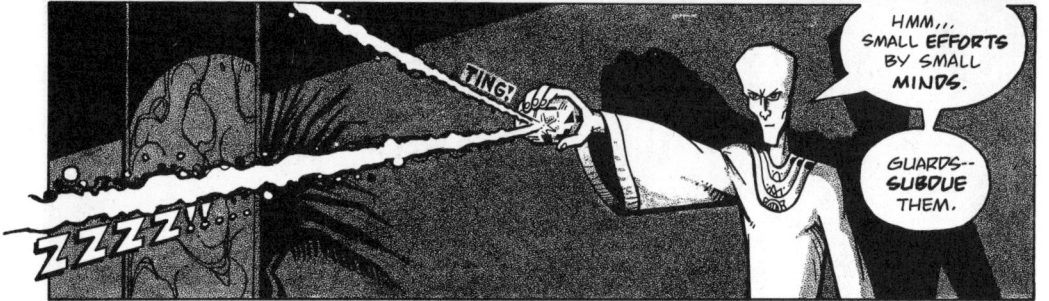

HMM... SMALL EFFORTS BY SMALL MINDS.

GUARDS-- SUBDUE THEM.

OOF! @★₤!! OUCH! WATCH IT! DAMN! AKK! OW!

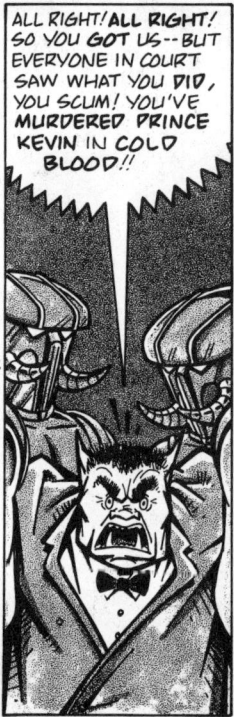

ALL RIGHT! ALL RIGHT! SO YOU GOT US-- BUT EVERYONE IN COURT SAW WHAT YOU DID, YOU SCUM! YOU'VE MURDERED PRINCE KEVIN IN COLD BLOOD!!

OH? AND IF I DID-- WHO WOULD PROSE-CUTE? YOU FORGET, MY DEAR IMBECILES, AS EMPEROR, I AM THE HIGHEST RANK-ING OFFICIAL ON THE PLANET.

I AM NOT ANSWERABLE TO ANYONE-- I AM ABOVE THE LAW.

ABOVE THE LAW PERHAPS, GEKKUS, BUT STILL BENEATH CONTEMPT!

...BUT **FIRST** LET ME **CONGRATULATE** YOU ON THAT **FINE BIT** OF SUPPOSED "**REGICIDE**."

CLAP
CLAP

BUT DON'T YOU THINK YOU SHOULD HAVE **CHECKED**...

"⚙" ?

...TO SEE IF THE "**PRINCE**" YOU KILLED WAS THE **GENUINE ARTICLE**?

KEVIN?

IN THE **FLESH!** AS OPPOSED TO THIS **SCOUTING ANDROID** I SENT TO THE MOON WITH YOU, GUARDS, **UNHAND** THEM.

AW, NOW **COME** ON! YOU MEAN WE'VE BEEN HANGIN' AROUND WITH A **MACHINE** ALL THIS TIME AND DIDN'T EVEN **KNOW** IT!

HAH! I'M **SURPRISED, MAX**—COULDN'T YOU "**TELL** BY ITS **VOICE**?"

I'LL MAKE THIS QUICK—YOU'VE BEEN UNDER **SURVEILLANCE** SINCE YOU AND **LIPPMAN** STOLE THE **JEWEL**...AND THE **SHIP** YOU STOLE WAS **PROGRAMMED** TO CRASH NEAR THE BUSH TOAD **TEMPLE**—I GAMBLED YOU'D FIND THE **JEWELS** ON YOUR **OWN**.

AS FOR THE **ANDROID**—IT WAS MY **EYES** AND **EARS THROUGHOUT** YOUR ENTIRE ADVENTURE...IT'S THE **STANDARD** PROCEDURE FOR INFORMATION RETRIEVAL WE "**ROYAL TYPES**" USE WHEN A MISSION IS TOO **RISKY** TO GO PERSONALLY.

GEKKUS WOULD HAVE **REALIZED** THAT, IF HE WASN'T SO **PREOCCUPIED** WITH MY "**DISAPPEARANCE**."

SPEAKING OF WHICH...

I'VE FLUSHED YOU **OUT**, **GEKKUS!** I KNEW IF YOU THOUGHT I WASN'T AT COURT YOU WOULD SHOW YOUR **TRUE COLORS!**

BUT NOW THE TABLES ARE **TURNED!!** I ACCUSE YOU OF **TREASON!** FOR CHALLENGING MY **RIGHTFUL** CLAIM OF SUCCESSION!!

I ACCUSE YOU OF **BLASPHEMY!** FOR USING THE **HOLY** ORDER OF THE GEM FOR YOUR OWN POLITICAL ENDS!!

AND I ACCUSE YOU OF **MURDER!!**...THE MURDER OF MY **FATHER**, THE **EMPEROR!!**

HIS BLOOD IS ON **YOUR** HANDS!!

83

INSOLENT FOOL! DO YOU SUPPOSE I HAVE COME THIS FAR TO BE STOPPED BY THE LIKES OF YOU!?!

AN EMPIRE'S RICHES ARE AT STAKE. I WILL NOT BE DENIED!

"AFTER HIM!!"

OUT ON A LIMB NOW, GEKKUS? CAN'T YOU SEE YOUR LUCK HAS RUN OUT?

STAY BACK, KEVIN! I STILL HAVE THE JEWEL! STAY BACK! I'M WARNING YOU!!

YOU'RE WARNING ME!?! GEKKUS, YOU FOOL! YOU DON'T REALIZE THE JEWEL'S TRUE POWER! IT CAN'T HELP YOU NOW!!

THE CURSE, GEKKUS... THE CURSE WON'T...

SILENCE!! THIS RELIGIOUS FARCE HAS GONE ON LONG ENOUGH! THERE IS NO CURSE, YOU IGNORANT WHELP! THAT WAS YOUR FATHER'S IDEA...TO PROP UP A MANUFACTURED THEOLOGY TO KEEP HIM IN POWER! IT'S JUST A STONE! A RADIOACTIVE STONE!!

GUARDS-- PREPARE TO FIRE!

N-NO!.. NO!!.. MY PLANS! MY DREAMS.!!..

HALT!!
OR FACE THE FULL FORCE OF POWERS HITHERTO UNKNOWN!!
I AM THE TRUE KEEPER OF THE GEM!!..
I.. AND I ALONE AM ITS GUARDIAN!! THERE IS NO CURSE!!! THERE IS N...
AAA!

AAAAAAAAAAAAAAA

AAAAAAAAAAAAAA

AAAAA✲

"MY GOD."

THUNK!

WHEW! *GOD* IS RIGHT, GUYS!.. I THINK WE JUST SAW **DIVINE INTERVENTION** AT ITS FINEST!

THEN... THE **CURSE**... WASN'T JUST A **GIMMICK** AT **ALL**, BUT... **REAL**?

REAL ENOUGH TO TURN GEKKUS INTO **FRICASEED ARISTOCRAT!**

AYE, THE CURSE WAS **REAL** ENOUGH...

GEKKUS SAW ONLY THE JEWEL'S **POLITICAL POWER**... IT WAS POWER HE CRAVED-- THE POWER **RELIGION** HAS TO CONTROL PEOPLE.

IT NEVER **OCCURED** TO HIM THAT **THIS** TIME IT MIGHT BE **LEGITIMATE**.

HMMM... IT'S OVERSIGHTS LIKE **THAT** THAT CAN RUIN YOUR **WHOLE DAY!**

RUIN YOUR DAY **AND** CHANGE THE **FATE** OF AN **EMPIRE**, EH, **KEVIN**?

PERHAPS, MY FRIENDS, PERHAPS, IF I CAN COUNT ON **YOUR** HELP.

AND I THOUGHT HE'D NEVER ASK!

FiNiTO, AMiGOS!

87

COVER GALLERY ►

During its run in **Threat!**, the
Holo. Brothers series was cover
featured three times. Here, in
the interests of completeness,
are those JIM ROHN illustrations,
sans colors and logos.

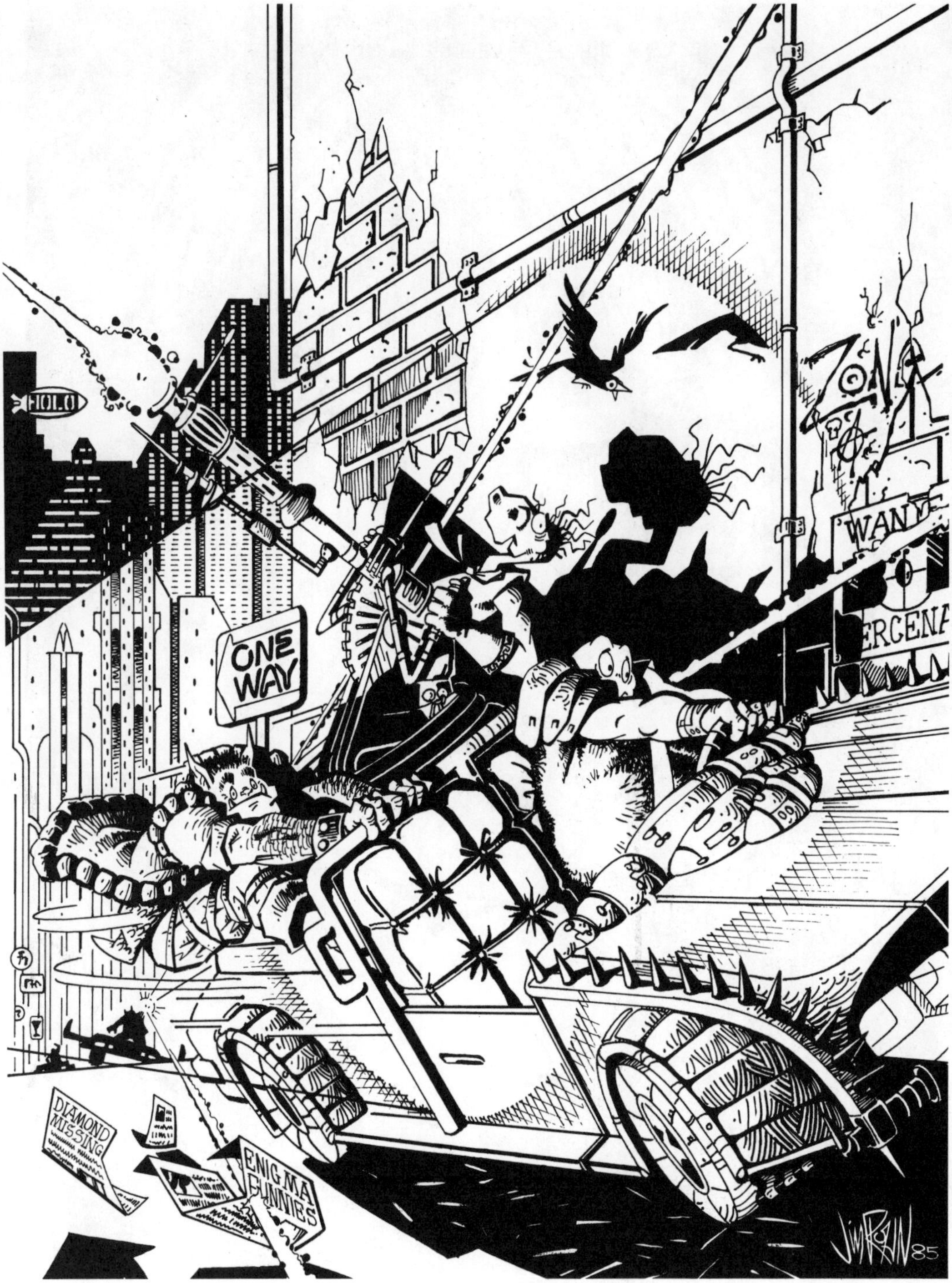
HOLO
ONE WAY
DIAMOND MISSING
ENIGMA FUNNIES